Do Animals Have Rights?

Yolanda Brooks

ARCTURUS

This edition first published by Arcturus Publishing
Distributed by Black Rabbit Books
P.O. Box 3263
Mankato
Minnesota MN 56002

Library of Congress Cataloging-in-Publication Data

Brooks, Yolanda.
  Do animals have rights? / Yolanda Brooks.
      p. cm. -- (Global questions)
ISBN 978-1-84837-010-4
1. Animal rights--Juvenile literature. I. Title.

HV4708.B756 2009
179'.3--dc22

2008016662

9 8 7 6 5 4 3 2

Series concept: Alex Woolf
Editor and picture researcher: Patience Coster
Designer: Ian Winton

Picture credits:
Corbis: 6 (Will Burgess/X00331/Reuters), 8 (Hulton-Deutsch Collection), 10 (Craig Holmes/Loop Images), 12 (Jose Fuste Raga/Zefa), 14 (Charles Platiau/Reuters), 17 (Ariel Skelley), 19 (Gyeongsang National University/HO/epa), 21 (Jason Szenes/epa), 27 (Martin Harvey), 29 (Jeff J. Mitchell/Reuters), 32 (Everett Kennedy Brown/epa), 33 (Paul Darrow/Reuters), 34 (Justin Lane/epa), 37 (Andy Mills/Star Ledger), 38 (Baverel Didier/Corbis Sygma), 40 (Bettmann), 41 (Felix Ordonez Ausin/Reuters), 42 (Juan Carlos Ulate/Reuters), 43 (Andy Clark/Reuters). Getty Images: 26 (Sonny Tumbelaka/AFP). Mary Evans Picture Library: 7. Rex Features: 25 (WSPA), 30. Shutterstock: 9, 13, 16, 22, 24, 28, 31, 35, 36, 39. Science Photo Library: 11 (Curt Maas/Agstockusa).

Cover: Calves on a dairy farm in Cambridgeshire, UK, recently separated from their mothers to encourage milk production (Gideon Mendel/Corbis).

Every attempt has been made to clear copyright. Should there be any inadvertent omission, please apply to the publisher for rectification.

Contents

Chapter 1

What do we mean by animal rights?

Whether or not animals should have rights is a hot topic of debate. While the concept of animal welfare is recognized as law in many countries, the issue of animal rights is much more controversial.

Rights versus welfare

People who support animal welfare are opposed to animal cruelty and seek ways to promote humane methods of looking after animals. Whether on a farm, in a laboratory, in the wild, or at home, animals should be free from fear and pain.

Animal rights advocates believe it is time to take a more radical approach to the way we think about and treat animals. For animal rights supporters, being animal friendly is not enough. They say that animals should have moral rights, like humans, because they can feel pain and experience suffering. Activists want animals to live free from human interference and exploitation.

Animal activists in Sydney, Australia, protest against the cramped conditions of the battery hen system by posing in a cage. The protesters said the hens were forced to lay eggs in a cruel environment.

If governments passed strict animal rights laws, we would no longer be able to treat animals as our property. They would have an automatic right to life and be free to live as nature intended. Hunting or farming animals for food or clothing would be illegal, the use of animals in any type of research would be banned, and we would no longer be able to keep animals as pets. Medical companies would need to find alternatives to animal testing, and zoos, aquariums, and animal circuses would close.

Crimes of compassion?

Donald Currie is an animal rights activist from Bournemouth in the United Kingdom (UK). He is a vegan and says he cares passionately about animals. He is also serving 12 years in prison for a bombing-and-arson campaign that targeted people who had connections with an animal-testing facility. In a letter from prison, he says: "I hate injustice, which is why I am opposed to animal abuse. To me, abuse against someone because of their race, color or beliefs is unacceptable. I extend this to every living creature." Some people believe that Donald Currie is a prisoner of conscience who has committed "crimes of compassion." To many others, he is an extremist or even a terrorist.

Getting the message across

Whether they believe in animal welfare or rights, most people who dedicate their lives to improving the well-being of animals use a variety of traditional and legal tactics. These include signing petitions, writing to local politicians or newspapers, going on protest marches, boycotting specific consumer goods and companies, and giving or raising money for animal protection charities and campaign organizations. A tiny minority of people are prepared to break the law by taking direct action against individuals and organizations they believe are guilty of abusing animals. These activists use a range of strategies: releasing animals from captivity, writing threatening letters, vandalizing fast-food restaurants, and spraying graffiti on billboards that feature cosmetics companies. They may publish names and addresses on the Internet to encourage house-to-house protests against people involved in animal abuse. In rare circumstances, animal rights activists have carried out attacks on people.

St. Francis of Assisi, the patron saint of animals, was an advocate for animals about 800 years before the concept of animal rights was born.

The birth of animal rights

Today many countries around the world have animal protection laws to prevent cruelty or extinction, but no laws exist to give individual rights to animals. Before the 1970s, there was no unified animal rights movement. A number of organizations campaigned and took action against specific activities. In the UK, for example, members of the Hunt Saboteurs Association tried to disrupt fox and stag hunts. In Canada, angry citizens launched the International Fund for Animal Welfare and took to the ice floes off the east coast to try to stop the annual seal pup cull.

While these individual groups were protesting, academics and philosophers were developing new theories about the relationship between humans and animals.

Speciesism

In the early 1970s, British psychologist and philosopher Richard D. Ryder invented the term *speciesism*. This is defined as prejudiced behavior toward animals. Most people display this type of behavior simply because they believe that humans are a superior species. Ryder argues that humans are not naturally superior to other animals and have no moral right to discriminate against them or cause them pain.

In March 1980, British actress Joanna Lumley and a group of volunteers stood outside 10 Downing Street in London, the home of the prime minister, with a petition calling for the British government to ban the import of Canadian seal products.

In 1975, a book titled *Animal Liberation* brought the issue of animal rights into the mainstream. Written by Australian academic Peter Singer, it set out the animal rights agenda and exposed the widespread abuse of animals in society. *Animal Liberation* has been described as the "starting pistol" for the animal rights movement, and since its publication hundreds of animal rights organizations have formed around the world. While they share a basic philosophy, each group has different views on exactly what the rights of animals should be.

Although there are few animal rights laws, activists have influenced consumer buying habits and brought about the introduction of tougher animal welfare laws. They have achieved this by raising awareness and through political lobbying. Animal rights campaigners have also had an influence on some traditional animal welfare organizations. Such organizations now campaign against animal abuse issues that were once only championed by animal rights groups. Supporters believe that in time, animal rights campaigns will become as influential as the social movements that saw the abolition of the transatlantic slave trade or that lobbied to win women the vote, or that fought to gain full civil rights for African Americans.

Some activists are campaigning for legal rights for great apes, such as gorillas, to give them greater protection and status above other animals.

FORUM

While some people believe animals should have rights, others think giving rights to animals will limit the rights of humans:

"Animal rights people find it inexcusable to accept that you can treat animals badly just because they happen to be different."

Ingrid Newkirk, co-founder and president of People for the Ethical Treatment of Animals

"To claim that man's use of animals is immoral is to claim that we have no right to our own lives and that we must sacrifice our welfare for the sake of creatures who cannot think or grasp the concept of morality."

Edwin A. Locke, professor of Leadership and Motivation, University of Maryland

What do you think?

Chapter 2

Can animal rights and farming co-exist?

Animal rights activists argue that intensive livestock farming is inhumane. They say farm animals endure miserable, stressful lives, suffer horrible deaths, and in the process are treated as inanimate objects rather than living, feeling beings. So is it possible to farm in an animal-friendly way?

Hens kept in free-range systems have the freedom to roam, forage for food, and follow their instincts.

Factory farming
The farming industry's main priority is the rapid production of cheap food, whatever the cost to animals. The aim of intensive farming is to produce large quantities of meat, eggs, and milk in the smallest space at the lowest cost. It is highly mechanized and requires the mass confinement of animals. The scale of the operation and the focus on efficiency means that this method of farming is often referred to as factory farming.

Meat, eggs, and milk have become more affordable as a result of intensive farming, and it has given people in developed countries access to a regular source of food. However, animal rights advocates say we cannot ignore the fact that modern farming methods brutalize billions of animals every day.

Flesh factories
Animal advocates point out the horrific aspects of intensive livestock farming. Chickens have their beaks removed and pigs' tails are chopped off without anesthetic. Because they have no commercial use, billions of male chicks are killed by crushing, gassing, or suffocation the moment they hatch. In some countries, male calves, an unwanted

product of the dairy industry, are taken from their mothers and fattened artificially in veal crates. Cruel slaughterhouse practices cause extra pain and stress.

Billions of animals endure very restricted lives. Pregnant pigs, for example, are kept indoors in gestation crates or stalls with metal bars and concrete floors. Before they give birth, the pigs are transferred to small farrowing crates. They can usually stand up and sit down, but they cannot turn around. They suckle their young for a few weeks, then are artificially impregnated and returned to the stalls.

FOCUS

Life in a cage

Most of the world's 5.6 billion hens live in battery systems, where tens of thousands of them are packed into wire cages. Several hens share a cage, so they cannot spread their wings or exhibit their natural behavior. They are routinely de-beaked to stop them pecking one another to death. The wire floors damage their feet, and the high egg production depletes the hens' calcium levels, causing osteoporosis and broken bones. British celebrity chef Jamie Oliver, who made the television series *Jamie's Fowl Dinners,* says: "It's simple. You get what you pay for. Cheap eggs mean lower welfare and worse conditions for hens."

Foul practices?

Broiler chickens are now bred to grow twice as fast as they did 30 years ago. Their legs can scarcely support their unnatural body weight, and the birds often experience skeletal disorders and heart and lung diseases. They suffer from blisters and eye infections caused by the buildup of droppings in the sheds where they are kept.

Battery cages are the ultimate intensive-farming method. Thousands of birds are caged in a small space in a controlled environment to maximize the number of eggs produced.

Milking machines

In 1970, the average dairy cow in the UK produced 975 gallons (3,750 liters) of milk a year. By 1995, a single cow could produce 1,650 gallons (6,345 liters) a year—an increase of almost 60 percent. These amazing increases in yield have been repeated in intensive-farming systems all over the world and are achieved through a combination of selective breeding, a high-energy protein diet, and medication. Dairy cows give birth to their first calves at about two years of age. One or two days after birth, the milking begins. The cow needs to be impregnated every year in order to keep producing milk. As a result, dairy cows often suffer from mastitis. Their high milk yields cannot be sustained for more than three or four years, so the animals are slaughtered long before they reach the end of their natural life span.

Misery on the move

Animal rights advocates point out that the suffering does not end at the farm. Animals are transported to slaughter or to other facilities for fattening. Animals in transit endure cramped conditions for days at a time and long stretches without food and water. Poor ventilation means that they suffer from extremes of heat or cold, and thousands of animals die or are injured in transit. Activists want limits on the transportation time of livestock to slaughterhouses, and they want to end the long-distance transportation of animals between farms.

Free-range alternatives

One way to improve welfare standards is to use organic and free-range farming systems. Instead of crates, cages, and indoor yards without bedding, the free-range, organic alternative consists of spacious enclosures and natural, healthier diets. With free-range systems, animals have access to daylight and the freedom to roam and express their natural behavior.

Farm animals are at risk from suffocation, stress, and changing temperatures during long-distance journeys that can last for several days without food, water, or rest.

Buffalo live freely and are slaughtered quickly when raised on organic ranches such as the Rocky Mountain Buffalo Ranch in British Columbia, Canada.

The main purpose of organic farming is to improve food quality. However, because animals are reared in more natural environments, their welfare also improves. In true organic farm systems, growth hormones are banned, which means that animals do not grow too quickly or too big. Organic farmers are not allowed to use drugs routinely to prevent the spread of disease. They therefore need to keep their animals healthy by giving them more space in which to live. This is one reason why many agricultural experts say it is not economically viable or possible to produce the same amount of meat and eggs using traditional free-range or organic systems.

FOCUS

Slaughter laws

Buffalo farmer Leo Downey runs an organic ranch in the Canadian Rocky Mountains. His buffalo roam free all year round, and when the time comes to slaughter them, he kills them quickly in the field with a bullet in the head. New government regulations mean that Leo will have to stop slaughtering the animals in this way and must transport them to a government-inspected slaughterhouse instead. He says: "To me the new laws are draconian [harsh] and really wrong. Putting the animals in a truck and hauling them for six hours to a plant is stressful for the animals. Our way is the least stressful and most humane way."

Animal-friendly living

For many activists, even the best welfare standards do not make up for the fact that, in their view, it is unacceptable to kill an animal for human consumption. Many of them insist that a strict vegan lifestyle is essential for anyone who supports the aims of the animal rights movement. Such a lifestyle involves a diet free of meat, fish, eggs, dairy produce, and even honey. Vegans shun honey because they believe it belongs to the bees that make it. Commercial production of honey also forces bees to live in unnatural conditions. Vegans refuse to use or wear leather, silk, and wool and regard the huge range of items containing animal by-products as off-limits.

Uncompromising animal rights supporters are sometimes very critical of animal welfare organizations and companies promoting cruelty-free products. They say that schemes such as the Freedom Food label in the UK and the Animal Welfare Approved stamp in the United States encourage the belief that cruelty-free farming is truly possible.

Animal rights revolution

If animal agriculture were banned, many practical problems would need to be overcome. Critics of the animal rights view say that if animal slaughter were made

Protesters from People for the Ethical Treatment of Animals (PETA) take inspiration from Renaissance artist Leonardo da Vinci as they offer vegetarian burgers to visitors to the Louvre Museum in Paris. According to PETA, Da Vinci was a vegetarian. Two of the protesters wear masks of da Vinci's famous painting, the *Mona Lisa*, and hold posters urging people to give up eating meat.

HAPPY BIRTHDAY LEONARDO! GO VEGETARIAN GoVeg.com

illegal, there would be billions of farm animals in the world. Where and how would we keep them? If they were set free, how would we prevent them from eating all the available vegetation? What would be the impact of the swelling numbers of wild predators who would find easy pickings from an abundant new food source? How would delicate habitats and ecosystems be affected by these changes?

Humans have been domesticating agricultural animals for at least 10,000 years, and many of today's farm animals bear little resemblance to their wild ancestors. These animals have no natural habitat to return to and so would probably need to be placed in sanctuaries. The average farm animal has been genetically selected to satisfy market demands. But the characteristics that mean an animal can be turned into a useful product at a supermarket might also lead to genetic weaknesses and an early and painful death if the creature were allowed to live out its life naturally.

In response to these arguments, animal rights supporters insist that if everyone became vegan, the world would not be overrun with hungry farm animals. They argue that if more people opted for a cruelty-free lifestyle, there would be less demand for meat and other animal products. Farmers would therefore breed fewer animals, and, over time, numbers would naturally decline. Farms would still exist to grow crops, and new industries dedicated to generating animal-free products would be created. Activists admit that there would be huge challenges, but they believe that the end of livestock farming would lead to a fairer, more ethical world for all animals.

FORUM

Some people think animals are put on this earth for humans to use as they like. Other people believe that justice for animals is long overdue.

"Eating a plate of food that contains no animal product of any kind marks you down as a squirrel. Eating only vegetables is like deciding to talk using only consonants. You need vowels or you make no sense."

Jeremy Clarkson, TV newscaster and newspaper columnist

"Rhetoric about how the public isn't ready for vegetarianism has got to be replaced by active promotion of the peaceful palate and equal justice for all animals."

Karen Davis, president of United Poultry Concerns

Which view do you agree with?

Chapter 3

Should animals be used for research?

Animal research and testing ignites fierce debate. Millions of animals are used in biomedical research to find cures for disease and to develop effective and safe drugs. Animals are also used in safety tests for many things, from food and cosmetics to household cleaning products and veterinary drugs. Organizations that conduct animal experiments include universities, pharmaceutical companies, medical research institutions, and the military.

Rodents such as rats are the most commonly used animals in laboratories because they are cheap to house. They have a short life span and so can be studied over several generations.

Facts and figures

The latest figures from the European Union (EU) reveal that just over 12 million animals a year are used in research. In Canada, the figure is much lower, 2.5 million. There are no official government figures for tests in the United States, but the Foundation for Biomedical Research estimates that between 17 and 23 million animals are involved. No figures are kept for invertebrates used in research.

The annual research and development statistics from the UK Home Office indicate the types of animals used in testing. Of the 3 million or more scientific procedures carried out in the UK in 2006, 83 percent used rodents such as rats, guinea pigs, or mice; 13 percent involved fish and birds; and less than 1 percent used dogs, cats, horses, and non-human primates. Other animals used in research included farm animals, reptiles, and amphibians.

Cruel or a necessary evil?

Animal rights abolitionists want to end all vivisection—their preferred term for animal experimentation. They claim the practice is not only cruel but also scientifically unproven. Governments and the scientific community disagree and insist that animal testing is essential for human safety, medical cures, and the advancement of scientific knowledge. They believe the way forward is the three Rs policy: reduction, refinement, and replacement. By this gradual process, they aim to improve animal welfare and limit the numbers of animals needed for research. Many welfare groups who view animal testing as a "necessary evil" support the three Rs policy.

Expert View

Some experts have no doubt that human life is more important than the lives of other animals:

"Those of us who research with animals, or support the benefits of such work, have made a moral choice. We place human well-being and health above that of animals and we unequivocally believe that human life comes first."

Stuart Derbyshire, senior lecturer in psychology, University of Birmingham, UK

For the last 30 years, undercover investigations and campaigns by animal rights groups have exposed the work carried out in animal-testing laboratories. Animal rights activists have focused on the way animals are treated, have described gruesome details of particular tests, and have questioned the effectiveness of animal experimentation. In doing so, they have influenced public opinion and put the issue of animal use in research on the political agenda.

Inoculation is a vital defense against many childhood illnesses. All vaccines are tested on animals to ensure their safety and effectiveness before they are given to humans.

Standards of care

In most countries, the law requires the testing of new drugs, products, and chemicals on animals. However, governments also have laws that set minimum standards of care for laboratory animals. These regulations do not ban painful experiments because experiments without anesthetic may be necessary to achieve accurate results.

In the UK and Australia, testing facilities need a license to do individual experiments, and government officials visit UK labs regularly. In the United States, birds, rats, and mice, the animals most commonly used in research, are excluded from the country's Animal Welfare Act and so have very limited legal protection.

The application of science

Thousands of different tests are done on animals. In biomedical research, for example, animals are infected with human diseases so that scientists can monitor the course of the illnesses. In transplantation studies, primates are implanted with tissue and organs from different species. Thousands of animals undergo surgical procedures and trials to test new medical equipment.

Genetic engineering is a growing area of research. Dozens of animal species have been cloned, and scientists carry out gene manipulation on animals to study how individual genes influence behavior and disease. They also transfer genes from one species to another to create transgenic animals.

The military uses animals such as pigs and primates to test the damage caused by weapons and to assess the effectiveness of battlefield clothing. Even dolphins are used in operations such as underwater mine

FOCUS

Looking for a cure

Oxford-based neurosurgeon Tipu Aziz conducts experiments on primates to find cures for disease. He brings about symptoms of Parkinson's disease either by surgically altering or by injecting their brains with a chemical. He then implants electrodes in their brains to alleviate the symptoms. Despite threats from animal rights activists, Aziz has no regrets about his methods. "You take someone who was bound to a wheelchair or unable to move and suddenly they have surgery based on conclusions drawn from my primate research and they are up again," says Aziz. "The animal rights extremists will have you see scientists as people who torture animals, but they don't give you the context."

Animal experimentation takes many forms: in December 2007, scientists in South Korea produced the kitten on the right by cloning, then manipulated its genes. As a result, it glows red in the dark when exposed to ultraviolet light, while a normal cat (seen on the left) does not.

clearance. In colleges and universities, animals are used in a wide range of situations, including dissection and behavioral studies.

Toxic shocks

Safety or toxicology testing is an area of research that provokes strong feelings among animal rights activists. In these tests, animals are dosed with products ranging from drugs and food additives to pesticides and cosmetics. Anesthetics are not used because they may affect the quality of the results.

The Draize and LD50 tests are two of the most controversial acute toxicity tests carried out in recent times. With LD50 (short for "lethal dose 50 percent"), researchers test a particular substance on a group of animals to find out the amount that is needed to kill 50 percent of them. With the Draize test, researchers repeatedly apply substances to an animal's eyes or skin to find out levels of irritation. After widespread protests, the use of these tests was limited and an alternative was found.

Activists argue that forcing animals to undergo painful procedures, often without pain relief, is unacceptable. They also say that giving human diseases to animals is wrong, as is keeping them in sterile, stressful conditions. All animals used in research are killed after they have been experimented on, and activists claim the methods of euthanasia used in laboratories are inhumane.

Bad science

Animal rights activists say experimentation not only causes great physical harm to the animals themselves but is of little value to human health. As proof, rights campaigners point to

FORUM

Some scientists believe that animal testing is essential, but others think it is unnecessary:

"Almost every major medical advance of the past hundred years has depended on animal testing. This includes organ transplantation; vaccines for diphtheria, polio, and meningitis; open-heart surgery; anesthetics; coronary bypass surgery; and drugs for high blood pressure, asthma, and leukemia."

Mark Matfield, director of the Research Defence Society

"In the 21st century, there is absolutely no need to torture and kill non-human animals to advance human medicine."

Jerry Vlasak, trauma surgeon and press officer for North American Animal Liberation

Which argument do you agree with?

tragedies that resulted from the use of the drug thalidomide in the 1950s and 1960s. Thousands of babies were born with deformed limbs and other serious birth defects after their mothers took the prescribed drug to stop morning sickness during pregnancy. Thalidomide had undergone limited animal testing.

More recently Vioxx, a popular painkiller used by arthritis sufferers, was taken off the market because its side effects included heart attacks and strokes. Vioxx had also been tested on animals. Animal rights groups claim that it is simply bad science to rely on results based on animal tests because animals are physically very different from humans. Instead, campaigners promote the use of alternatives such as micro-dosing. With this technique, human test subjects are injected with tiny amounts of a new drug to see how their bodies process it. The dose is so small that the drug only affects cells and not the whole body. In theory, once researchers understand how a tiny dose reacts in the body, they can begin to determine whether it is safe for additional testing.

While governments and research organizations have made some concessions to the animal welfare and rights movement, they remain convinced that without reliable alternatives, animal experimentation is essential for human health and the welfare of other animals.

In the name of beauty

How can it be argued that non-essential products, such as eye shadow and lipstick, need testing on animals? There is a range of opinions on this and regulations for animal tests for cosmetics vary from country to country. But the animal rights movement has made many consumers aware of the cruelty involved in cosmetics testing, and as a result, several governments have been persuaded to ban the practice. It is now unlawful in the Netherlands, Belgium, and the UK. From 2009, it will be illegal to produce or import cosmetics that have been tested on animals into the European Union.

These laws have been passed because politicians have been persuaded that cosmetics testing is a mainstream issue and that the majority of the public opposes animal testing. The huge and sustained campaigns that have led to the European Union ban will also affect cosmetics companies around the world. These businesses will have to change their testing policies if they want continued access to the lucrative European market. Companies such as L'Oreal and Proctor & Gamble, for example, have spent a combined $1.2 billion on alternative testing methods.

When The Body Shop was launched in 1976, its selection of cruelty-free products was seen as a novelty. Today, The Body Shop is owned by the huge cosmetics company L'Oreal, which, despite its research into alternative methods, continues to test on

animals. While this situation has angered some ethical shoppers, cruelty-free cosmetics are now generally available in most mainstream stores, including supermarkets and drugstores, so buying ethically is easier than it used to be.

Cruelty-free cosmetics are not just an ethical choice but a legal requirement in countries that have banned animal testing for cosmetics.

Chapter 4

Is conservation good for animal rights?

Animal rights activists believe that all living creatures are entitled to equal rights and respect. The common sewer rat is as important as the rare and endangered panda. Animal rights activists believe that all animals deserve lives free from cruelty. And while some humans may value certain species above others, activists say that this should not influence the way all species are treated.

Arguments about intervention

Animal rights activists care more about individual animals than whole species, which means they do not always see eye to eye with conservationists. Conservationists are more concerned with biodiversity; in other words, the number and balance of different plants and animals within a particular habitat. If a particular animal threatens the biodiversity of a particular area, the conservationists' main concern is to find ways to ensure that the various species can survive and co-exist. They look at the requirements of species as a whole rather than worrying about the needs of individual animals. Conservationists also want to prevent the extinction of species. Their methods of keeping species alive might involve the control of other animals by culling or other means.

Zoos around the world run breeding programs for the threatened sun bears of Southeast Asia, which are hunted for meat and medicine.

FOCUS

Compassion and conservation

Jane Goodall is a world expert on chimpanzees. She believes that compassion for animals can exist alongside conservation and human development. Goodall became famous in the 1960s for her research work with wild chimpanzees in Tanzania. In 1977, she set up the Jane Goodall Institute, which runs Roots and Shoots, a global youth project that combines humanitarian, conservation, and wildlife activism. She says: "Confrontation can be counterproductive. Change happens by listening and then starting a dialogue with the people who are doing something you don't believe is right."

Many animal rights groups would prefer it if humans left nature to take its course. Conservationists say the hands-off approach may sound reasonable in theory, but its effects will harm the very animals the rights groups want to protect. Not only will these animals face slow death through starvation, but they could become extinct if conservationists are not allowed to intervene.

Selective poisoning

The Western Shield predator control project in Australia is a good example of how the interests of conservationists and animal rights advocates come into conflict. Feral cats and red foxes have wreaked havoc with native wildlife in Australia. They prey on small mammals and reptiles, and as a result, several species are now close to extinction. In 1996, the Western Australian government launched a huge conservation project to combat the problem.

The project was called Western Shield, and it set out to cull the cats and foxes with poisoned bait. (The species these animals preyed on are immune to this particular poison.) A huge baiting program was launched. Every three months, 77,000 pieces of bait were dropped from aircraft across 1.4 million acres (3.5 million hectares) of Western Australia.

The plan was seen as a great success, and pest species died in large numbers, while endangered animals such as wallabies, western swamp tortoises, and rat kangaroos flourished. But animal rights supporters protested that the poison killed not only feral cats and foxes but other species too. The animals were said to suffer a "protracted and cruel" death. The poison is still being used throughout Australia and New Zealand, but animal rights supporters are campaigning hard to ban it. They believe the poison not only kills non-target species but also poses risks to the environment and to human health.

Life behind bars

Zoos that run captive breeding programs present another ethical dilemma for animal rights supporters. While conceding that many programs are set up with good intentions, animal rights activists argue that zoos really exist to entertain the public and their conservation and education activities are simply a sideline to this main event. Animal rights supporters question the ethics of zoos that are more interested in breeding the "superstar" species such as tigers, bears, and elephants. They say the reason for this is that these species provoke public interest and bring in revenue to the zoo. Meanwhile, other equally deserving but less photogenic animals remain a lower priority.

Przewalski horses were extinct in the wild until a successful international captive-breeding program led to their re-introduction to Mongolia.

If zoos are genuinely concerned about endangered species, say activists, they could run breeding programs away from the public eye on large habitat reserves. This would give the animals the freedom of movement they need and a more natural environment away from humans. Animal rights advocates believe that many captive-breeding programs simply drain existing wild populations. When zoos remove animals from their natural environment, they reduce the number of healthy animals left to breed in the wild. Activists also point out that without concerted efforts to preserve habitat, zoos will simply become permanent "arks" for animals that have no real hope of returning to the wild.

Fair game or cruel food?

Although they have many differences to overcome, the animal rights and environmental movements share many beliefs. When animals lose their natural habitat or die through hunting and trafficking, their rights are being ignored. Animal rights activists campaign to stop these abuses because they believe the most important thing is to prevent cruelty to individual animals.

Thousands of great apes are killed for food each year in Africa. Some animals are killed by poor people who have limited access to other food sources, but many more are snared or shot by poachers involved in the commercial trade of bushmeat. The activity also fuels the trade in primates as pets. Young apes are too small to be worth killing for meat, so poachers sell them as pets. Those that escape the poachers face starvation.

Bushmeat on sale: African wildlife, including apes, antelopes, crocodiles, and elephants, is considered fair game by people who hunt for profit and those who eat bushmeat to stay alive.

Animal rights activists protest against the controversial bushmeat trade, not because they think that eating apes and other wild animals places them under threat of extinction but because they believe that capturing and killing any animal causes great suffering. Conservationists, on the other hand, campaign against the bushmeat trade because it is causing primate numbers to fall rapidly.

FOCUS

Breeding disaster

In 2006, Knut the polar bear cub was born in the Berlin Zoo. He was rejected by his mother and rescued by zookeepers, who hand-reared him. Knut became a huge international celebrity, but he is now so used to human contact that he cannot be returned to the wild. A few months after Knut was born, two polar bears at the Nuremberg Zoo gave birth to cubs. Trying to avoid a repeat of "Knut-mania," the keepers took a hands-off approach. Unfortunately, two of the cubs were eaten by the mother. Like many wild animals, polar bears are difficult to breed in captivity. Even with the best facilities, it can be a struggle to produce the healthy offspring needed for the long-term survival of a species.

Trade in wild birds

In 2006, dozens of animal welfare, animal rights, and environmental organizations joined one another in lobbying the European Union to legislate for a permanent ban on the commercial import of wild birds. The EU was already considering a ban because of fears about the spread of "bird flu." Conservation groups were worried about the indiscriminate hunting of birds, which was reducing the numbers of certain species, and animal rights and welfare groups focused their attention on the cruelty of the trade.

Between 2000 and 2003, almost 3 million wild-caught listed birds were imported into Europe. Traumatic capture methods and long-distance journeys around the world cause high fatality rates. The Environmental Investigation Agency has carried out years of undercover work on the trade in wild birds. It estimates that for every single bird that survives the journey, three others die.

Birds in a cramped cage for sale at the local market in Denpasar, Indonesia. The trade in exotic wild birds has a high casualty rate and threatens the numbers of certain bird species.

The collaboration of the various lobbying groups produced success, however. In July 2007, a wild bird trade ban came into effect in the EU (import bans were already in place in the United States, Canada, and Australia).

A charter for apes

In 1993, an international group of animal scientists and experts, animal rights activists, and academics signed the Declaration of Great Apes to launch the Great Ape Project. This project aims to give great apes increased legal protection and the right to life, liberty, and protection from torture. Activists from the group want the United Nations (UN) to draw up a declaration of rights for great apes.

Humans have a close genetic link with great apes, such as chimpanzees, gorillas, and orangutans. Research has also shown that great apes experience complex emotions and can communicate with humans. For these reasons, supporters of the Great Ape Project believe we should give great apes a status above that of other non-human animals.

Sometimes the rights of animals may conflict with the right to survival of certain species:

"If people are encouraged to believe that the harm done to animals matters morally *only when* these animals belong to endangered species, then these same people will be encouraged to regard the harm done to other animals as morally acceptable."

Tom Regan, animal rights philosopher

"Balancing conservation and responsible wildlife management is not done by animal rights people. Nature has a way of brutalizing itself with overpopulation, starvation and disease and who looks after that? When I trap a beaver or any other species, I feel good that I have provided the space and habitat for another healthy animal to replace it."

Reed Gauthier, fur trapper from Alberta, Canada

Where do you stand in the argument between animal rights supporters and conservationists?

While some animal advocates see this approach of granting rights to certain species as realistic and achievable, other rights groups believe that to start distinguishing "intelligent" or more deserving animals from others simply perpetuates speciesism. While great apes would be protected from hunting and animal research, there would be no such safeguards in place for other animals.

An orphan gorilla takes medicine from a keeper at a rehabilitation center in Africa. Gorillas are in danger of extinction because they are hunted for their meat and because their natural habitat in central Africa is rapidly disappearing.

Chapter 5

Should hunting be banned?

Unlike farm or companion animals, wild animals can roam freely and live as nature intended. Survival in the wild is harsh, but wild animals are not subjected to the cramped conditions or unnatural diets of their captive counterparts. Hunting helps to maintain healthy populations, and a skillful hunter can ensure the kill is swift. So why do animal rights activists object to hunting?

Problem predators

Animal rights activists say hunting is cruel, unnecessary, and bad for conservation. Inexperienced hunters may botch their shots so that animals endure lingering deaths. Animals suffer in agony for days in traps before the hunters find, release, and then kill them. Also, for the hunted animals the stress of the chase prolongs suffering, young animals are orphaned, and family groups are destroyed.

Hunting may no longer be a matter of survival in the West but it is still a popular pastime enjoyed by millions of people.

As far as conservation goes, animal advocates say the pastime has caused the extinction of several species and threatened the long-term survival of many others. In the 1970s and 1980s, the African elephant faced extinction because it was hunted in huge numbers for its ivory. Numbers began to recover only after the international sale of ivory was banned. Today bear hunting is allowed in some eastern European countries despite the fact that brown bears are a threatened species in Europe.

A human right

Hunting is essentially a pastime carried out by individuals, which means that animal rights activists cannot blame governments and big business for any cruelty or suffering caused to hunted animals. The activists need to direct their appeal to the hunters themselves.

Hunters in developed countries believe that the right to hunt is a matter of personal choice. However, the UK government has recently banned the traditional field sports of fox hunting and hare coursing in England and Wales (the Scottish parliament already banned them). After many years of campaigning and parliamentary debates, hunting with dogs was banned because of the cruelty involved. Following the ban, a number of pro-hunt organizations appealed to the courts, claiming that the new laws were unconstitutional because people's human rights were being violated. According to the European Convention on Human Rights, they said, the anti-hunting laws removed their right to a certain way of life and their right to earn a living. The appeal failed, however, and the hunters have had to find alternative ways to keep their tradition alive.

FOCUS

Seal hunting

Far north in Canada, in the territory of Nunavut, Inuit communities hunt seals for food and use their pelts for clothing and in arts and crafts. The Inuit take about 30,000 seals a year, which they say is a sustainable number. They also argue that they kill the seals in a humane way, with rifles. Sales of fur pelts and other seal by-products allow the people of Nunavut to continue their traditional, land-based way of life. According to the Department of Economic Development and Transportation in Nunavut: "The anti-sealing lobby is viewed in the Arctic as a direct assault on culture, [and] identity, as well as sustainable use."

A scene from the recent past: a huntsman from the South Durham hunt in northern England holds up a fox that was shot after being flushed out of its hiding place by hounds. Traditional fox hunting has now been banned in the UK, and it is no longer legal to use dogs to chase or kill foxes.

Hunting for fun

Hunting is a popular pastime in the United States, and hunters are allowed to catch and kill everything from bighorn sheep and bears to buffalo and moose. An estimated 12.5 million hunters spend about $23 billion a year on equipment, licenses, hunting fees, club membership fees, travel, lodging, and food. It is also possible to hunt more exotic creatures at private ranches. Exotic trophy hunting is big business in Texas, where hunters pay thousands of dollars to track and kill animals such as zebra, giraffes, kudu, tapir, and sable. Some ranches run captive breeding programs from which they help replenish the stocks of wild herds in Asia and Africa. Others also give financial support to international conservation programs.

Wearing fur is controversial, but trapping animals for the fur trade is legal. Fashion designer Jean Paul Gaultier risks the wrath of the animal rights lobby by featuring animal skins in his 2008 collection.

Animal rights groups believe that hunters today are only interested in the thrill of the kill, not in conservation or enjoying the environment. Animal rights protesters have accused some ranches of running "canned hunts," where hunters track and kill semi-tame animals in enclosures and where there is little chance for the victims to escape. In the world of the modern hunter, major roads pass through wilderness areas and the chase is made much easier by technology such as night vision equipment and electronic decoys. Today hunting appears to be just another branch of the entertainment business.

In Italy, the hunting of wild birds is still popular. The birds are hunted and killed as they migrate, and animal rights activists claim that 17 million birds from 40 different species are legally killed in traps, in snares, and with guns between September and January every year. These activists point out that the EU laws governing bird hunting are poorly enforced. Many police forces turn a blind eye or do not have enough staff to enforce the laws that limit the species of birds killed. Animal rights activists say that as many as 10 million birds are killed illegally every year.

Expert View

Cultures differ in the type of animal they enjoy killing and eating:

"You can't hide the fact that whales belong to the animal kingdom, and as long as most people are prepared to eat other animals, then we can't see a big difference between eating whales and eating beef."

Rune Frovik of High North Alliance, a Norwegian pro-whaling group

Slaughter at sea

In the Faroe Islands in the North Atlantic, the local people have hunted pilot whales for generations. Records kept since the 1900s indicate that between 200 and 3,000 whales are killed every year. When a group of whales is spotted, the word is sent out to local communities, who gather on the beaches or take to the water to drive the whales ashore.

Once the animals have been herded into shallow waters, they are dragged farther onto dry land with steel hooks. Their spinal cords are severed with a knife, a practice that is supposed ensure a quick or at least a pain-free death. Even the government of the Faroe Islands admits that the hunts are a "dramatic and bloody sight." Most of the meat is distributed throughout the community, so nothing is wasted. However, Faroe Islanders no longer rely on whale meat for survival, and it is just one of many meat sources in their national diet.

A structure built of whale bones in the Faroe Islands provides a reminder of the country's whaling heritage.

Hunting for profit

Animal rights groups do not just target people who hunt for fun and tradition; they also direct their anger at some of those people who hunt for a living.

In 1985, the International Whaling Commission (IWC) halted the practice of commercial whaling. Despite this, hundreds of whales are still killed every year by fleets from countries such as

Local people from the Japanese whaling town of Wada look on as a Baird's beaked whale is prepared for slaughter.

Norway, Iceland, Japan, and Greenland. Some whales are killed for scientific purposes and others to supply the whale meat market. A few hundred whales are also killed by indigenous groups in North America. Modern whaling fleets kill whales with explosive harpoons. Animal rights and welfare activists say it takes too long for a whale to die by this method. They add that there is no humane way of killing a whale because the animals are too large to kill quickly.

Animal rights and welfare activists in countries including the UK, Australia, and New Zealand have put pressure on their governments to pass an international ban on whaling. Although the IWC was originally set up as a conservation body to preserve whaling stocks, many governments have been persuaded to vote against whaling on animal welfare grounds.

Blood on the ice

Every spring, animal rights activists arrive on the pack ice near the four Canadian provinces on the Atlantic coast to highlight the brutality of the seal pup culls. Undercover footage has shown animals dragged across the ice on hooks, being skinned alive, and being clubbed repeatedly. In recent years, the Canadian government has issued permits allowing hunters to kill up to 325,000 harp seals. The annual cull has been a major animal rights issue since the 1960s, and the gruesome-looking killing methods have persuaded many governments to ban the import of seal products.

Opinions vary about whether people have the right to take the life of an animal for food, fun, or tradition:

"It's perfectly permissible for people to dislike hunting; it's perfectly all right for them to try to persuade other people not to hunt. But what is not acceptable is for parliamentarians driven by bigotry and prejudice to try and use their position in parliament to enforce their moral opinion as a matter of law."

Richard Burge, Countryside Alliance, UK

"It cannot be right to slaughter an innocent animal in the name of sport."

Douglas Batchelor, League Against Cruel Sports, UK

What is your opinion?

Survival issues

For subsistence communities, hunting is not just a way of life, it is a matter of survival. Animal rights groups admit that some of these hunters live in impoverished circumstances and have little choice but to hunt. However, they believe that others, especially those in Western countries, have access to humane alternatives.

Ultimately, no matter how quick the kill, animal rights activists believe that hunting is ethically wrong because animals should not be exploited like a renewable resource. Even if survival in the wild is harsh, humans should take a hands-off approach to wildlife and allow nature to take its course.

A seal hunter collects carcasses from an ice floe in the Gulf of St-Lawrence in Canada during the annual seal cull.

Chapter 6

Is it cruel to keep companion animals?

Even if you do not keep a pet or a companion animal at home, you probably know someone who does. In the United States and Australia, 63 percent of households have at least one animal living with them. In the UK, 52 percent of families have a pet living with them, such as a dog, a cat, a bird, a fish, a reptile, or a rodent. Just counting the hounds and the felines, that adds up to 85 million dogs and 100 million cats in the United States, the UK and Australia alone.

American celebrity Paris Hilton has been accused of setting a bad example by treating her pets, which include a chihuahua, a ferret, and a kinkajou (rain forest mammal), as fashion accessories.

Expert View

Some animal experts say keeping pets is not a problem provided they are cared for properly:

"If you provide the best possible environment for your animal and enrich its life, it will enrich yours in turn and that is a good partnership. It's owners who don't know how to look after their pets, don't bother to find out, and couldn't care less who are unethical, in my view. Sadly, I see a lot."

David Grant, Royal Society for the Prevention of Cruelty to Animals vet

Animal lovers?

Pets keep us company, encourage us to be more active, and protect and entertain us. Numerous research studies have also shown that they are good for our health. In return, we invest a lot of money and time on their care. In the United States alone, people spend an estimated $41 billion a year on pet food, veterinary bills, and medicine, equipment, grooming services, toys, shelter, and temporary care. The majority of people with companion animals would describe themselves as animal lovers and see no problem with ownership as long as the animals are well cared for.

Not ours to own

Some animal rights advocates support the abolition of all forms of animal ownership. They say that to keep companion animals is to treat them as commodities. An animal can never have rights if it is the property of humans because it cannot choose when or what it eats or where it lives. It cannot exhibit its true personality if its behavior conflicts with its owner's interests. If an owner decides that he or she no longer wants the companion animal, it faces life in a shelter or death by gassing or lethal injection.

Other animal rights activists and welfarists support the view that keeping certain animals is ethical provided that we act as responsible owners. Not only should owners meet the individual needs of animals in their care, but they should make sure that their actions do not have a negative impact on other animals.

A running ball provides some much needed exercise for captive hamsters that would run up to two miles a day if they lived in the wild. Whether the animal enjoys the activity, however, is hard to say.

Problems with pets

Animal rights advocates agree that although companion animals enjoy "special status" and often have greater legal protection than farm or wild animals, keeping them creates significant welfare problems. General neglect by owners, routine cruel practices, strays and abandoned animals, overbreeding, ill health caused by inbreeding, and the keeping of exotic pets are all areas for concern.

Neglect and cruelty

While most owners look after their pets responsibly, there are people who neglect their animals' needs. For example, some chain their dogs for hours at a time; others leave animals to roam the streets, provide the wrong diet, offer inadequate shelter or do not bother to exercise their pets or give them a stimulating environment.

Animal shelters provide only a temporary refuge for animals that are often destroyed if new homes cannot be found.

Stray and unwanted animals are a huge problem because they face starvation, disease, and early death. They are more likely to be ill treated because they run wild and pose a danger to human health and safety. The World Society for the Protection of Animals estimates that there are 600 million dogs and almost as many cats in the world. Of these, it is estimated that 80 percent are stray or unwanted. Even in countries with strong animal welfare laws and a long tradition of pet ownership, there are too many dogs and cats, and as a result, shelters are filled with millions of unwanted animals. Some are adopted by new owners, but millions of others have to be destroyed.

Animal welfare and rights organizations believe that neutering a pet is one of the essential principles of responsible pet ownership. They also urge people to adopt pets from shelters rather than buy them from a pet store or commercial breeding facility.

Commercial breeding

Animal rights activists insist that commercial-breeding facilities make the overpopulation problem worse by producing animals for profit. The animals are often forced to live in grim conditions that affect their physical and psychological health. Dogs reared on puppy farms are kept in cramped, dirty cages and have few opportunities to socialize with humans. This means that they may be dangerous when later placed in family homes. Female dogs kept on puppy farms are bred continuously, which exhausts them and affects their health.

People differ in their views about the rights and wrongs of keeping companion animals:

"[Domesticated animals] are perpetually dependent on us. We control their lives forever. They truly are 'animal slaves.' We may be benevolent 'masters,' but we really aren't anything more than that. And that cannot be right."

Gary L. Francione, legal academic and animal rights theorist

"Animals, and nature in general, are a marvelous health tonic. If we include them in our lives, if our physiology is set in a way that includes the rest of the living world, then we shall live longer and certainly more rewarding lives."

James J. Lynch, psychologist and director of the Life Care Foundation

What is your view?

Exotic species

Humans have been domesticating cats and dogs for thousands of years, so these animals have adapted to live alongside people. Wild animals, however, are often difficult to train. They may be cute and cuddly when they are young but aggressive when they reach maturity, and they often need a large, extra-secure shelter to live in. Many owners do not understand the complex dietary and behavioral needs of exotic animals and end up letting them loose in the wild or handing them over to zoos or rescue sanctuaries.

A dog peers out of a hole in a door on a farm in Pennsylvania where puppies are bred to supplement the farmer's income. Dogs bred commercially are treated like farm animals, not pets.

Chapter 7

Should animals be used for entertainment?

For many people, animal entertainers are a source of harmless pleasure. These people sometimes perceive animal rights activists as killjoys who are simply trying to spoil the fun of others when they really should be concentrating on more serious animal abuse issues. But there are serious concerns when it comes to animals and entertainment. They range from captivity issues to activities such as bullfights and rodeos.

Live entertainment

Animal advocates are wary of institutions such as zoos, aquariums, and circuses. They believe that wild animals should be left in the wild. They say keeping a dolphin or a killer whale in a pool is like forcing a human to spend a lifetime in a bathtub. They condemn zoos because many of these institutions keep animals in unnatural environments that have been proven to damage their physical and psychological well-being.

Research has shown that animals grow bored in captivity. Without stimulation, many species display abnormal repetitive behavior such as rocking back and forth, licking the bars of their cage, pacing, and self-mutilation. While many zoos strive to create more stimulating animal enclosures and pay greater attention to the psychological aspects of animal care, others are not so responsible.

In the wild, elephants roam in large social groups. Performing circus animals spend much of their life on the road, confined to transporters, cages, or small exercise enclosures.

Dog agility competitions are a popular spectator sport. Judging by the enthusiasm of many of the dogs taking part, we might think animals enjoy them, but can we be sure they do?

The Zoo Check campaign singles out zoos in Thailand, Spain, Africa, Eastern Europe, and Southeast Asia for particular criticism. Photographs of zoos in these countries reveal small, barren enclosures with no place of refuge from prying eyes and with animals in poor physical condition.

Wildlife road show

Animal activists insist that wild animals should not be used in traveling circuses. They believe that the circus tricks performed by animals such as elephants and big cats undermine the animals' dignity and freedom and have no place in the modern world.

While circus trainers insist that they coach their animals using positive reinforcement techniques, animal rights groups have recorded training sessions on film that tell quite a different story. One trainer in a US circus is heard telling a trainee to "make 'em scream" as he demonstrates how to use a stick to coerce elephants. In the UK, undercover activists posed as trainees and caught experienced trainers beating chained animals with pitchforks and riding crops. Evidence from the investigation led to criminal convictions for cruelty.

Animal rights supporters believe that a normal, healthy existence is incompatible with life on the road and the sooner people stop paying money to see animals perform, the sooner the suffering will stop. Awareness campaigns have worked well in several countries, and only a handful of circuses in the UK, for example, still use animal performers.

Expert View

For some experts, using animals to entertain humans is clearly unacceptable:

"We can learn as much about lions by studying them in their captivity as we can about men by studying them in their prison cells."

Virginia McKenna, actress and trustee of the Born Free Foundation

Creature features

Animal actors may sometimes be pampered, but they are also exploited. In the 1939 Hollywood Western *Jesse James*, the hero and his horse jump off a cliff and fall 82 feet (25 meters) into a raging river. At the time, audiences were thrilled and amazed, until the truth came out. The horse had been blindfolded and a trip wire set at the cliff's edge. The stuntman survived the fall, but the horse broke its back and died.

In the following year, the American Humane Society set up a film-monitoring service to ensure the on-set safety of animals appearing in films. Although the society's stamp of approval appears at the end of most current

American performer and "Singing Cowboy" Gene Autry trains his horse for a routine. Back in the golden era of Hollywood, film sets used to be dangerous places for horses, but today animal welfare advisers try to ensure that performing animals are not harmed during filming.

Hollywood films in which animals are featured, some animal rights groups have criticized the film industry for its continued reliance on animals. They believe that on-set monitoring of animal safety is not rigorous enough to protect animals. Even if the stunts look safe and the animals are well cared for on set, it is relatively easy to hide abusive training regimes and unsuitable long-term living conditions from animal welfare advisers.

Hollywood film sets may be safer for animals today, but the use of animals in film is still unregulated in many countries. The UK film censors cut 18 seconds from the Chinese film *House of Flying Daggers* because they detected several instances of real animal cruelty during some spectacular horse chases. With the availability of animatronics, advanced special effects, and stock footage, animal rights groups point out that there is no longer any need to continue exploiting animals in film.

FOCUS

Free in name only

In 1992, a killer whale named Keiko starred in the Hollywood film *Free Willy*, about a boy who helps release a captive killer whale into the wild. *Free Willy* was a huge hit, but what the public did not know was that an underweight Keiko languished in his Mexican aquarium with lesions on his skin. A multi-million-dollar rescue mission was launched to try to release him back into the wild. Although he was finally freed from captivity, Keiko died in 2003 in a fjord in Norway while his handlers were still trying to rehabilitate him. During his life, Keiko had lived in four different aquariums and was twice transported across the Atlantic.

Dance of death

No animal protection organizations are willing to approve the bullfights held on a regular basis in Spain, Portugal, and Latin American countries. A bullfight features an unequal contest between an injured bull and a matador armed with a dagger. In a traditional Spanish bullfight, the bull first faces a picador on horseback. The picador jabs his lance (spear) into the neck of the animal to weaken its muscles and tire it out. Then the matador takes center stage. In a series of stylized moves, the matador tries to inflict a clean kill while making sure he is not gored by the horns of the angry bull. Animal advocates describe the activity as a "ritualistic dance of death." People who enjoy bullfighting say it is a traditional art that is also a display of human (usually masculine) skill and courage.

Wearing traditional dress, Spanish matador José Antonio Ferrera does battle with a bull during a bullfight at the El Plantio bullring in Burgos, northern Spain, in June 2007.

Rough riders

In the rodeos of the American and Canadian West, the fast, furious, and physical nature of the activities means that animals regularly lose their lives. At events such as the Calgary Stampede in Alberta, Canada, horses are raced hard, bulls are ridden rough, calves are roped, and steers are wrestled to the ground as modern-day cowboys and cowgirls show off their livestock-handling skills to enthusiastic crowds.

Animal rights activists are particularly concerned about events such as bareback riding and steer wrestling. They say the training involved is cruel to the animals and the use of implements such as electric prods and spurs adds to their distress. Collisions and the general rough-and-tumble of these activities cause lots of broken bones, and animals are regularly euthanized (destroyed) on-site.

A bull rider tries to gain the upper hand during an international tournament in San José, Costa Rica.

Activists say many of the events at rodeos are accidents waiting to happen. The chuck wagon races at Calgary have proved particularly dangerous for participating horses. Teams of four horses pull pioneer-style wagons at fast speeds in figure-eight formations. During the last decade, at least 15 horses have been killed during these races.

Making history

In the past, blood sports such as bear baiting and cockfighting were acceptable and legal. Animal rights groups believe many of the activities that are considered acceptable today will be regarded with horror and disgust in the future. With the knowledge we have about animal intelligence and sensibilities, animal rights groups say it is time to find other ways of amusing ourselves. They argue that animals are not put on earth to

In Ottawa, Canada, members of the International Fund for Animal Welfare (IFAW) dress in costumes of endangered animals, drawing attention to the threat to the existence of certain species.

entertain or educate humans, and they should not be used as sacrificial ambassadors for their species.

By rejecting out-of-date traditions and staying away from captive institutions, we can help ensure that animals will no longer be exploited for fun. For the animal rights supporters, animal rights philosophy is a way of thinking as well as doing. Only when we let go of old attitudes and beliefs will animals gain their freedom and achieve the real rights to which they are entitled.

FORUM

Some people think it is important to learn from captive animals, while others believe all animals should be free:

"While people can learn much about animals from books, movies, and the Internet, there is nothing that will open human eyes, minds, and hearts to these wonderful creatures more quickly and thoroughly than seeing an animal in the flesh and observing its behavior in a habitat display or with a trainer or handler."

National Animal Interest Alliance

"Those who wish to pet and baby wild animals 'love' them. But those who respect their natures and wish to let them live normal lives love them more."

Edwin Way Teal, naturalist and author

Which view do you agree with?

Glossary

activist A person who works to create change by political campaigning, raising awareness, or direct action.

advocate A person who defends or supports a particular cause.

animal rights A belief system that opposes the exploitation of animals for any reason. Also referred to as animal liberation.

animal rights abolitionist A person who believes animals should not be treated as property and who wants to end all exploitation of sentient creatures.

animal welfare A principle that accepts the use of animals but demands compassionate and humane treatment to ensure that they live a life free from pain and cruelty and do not suffer physical or psychological harm.

animatronics Special effects using mechanized puppets.

arson The act of deliberately setting fire to a building.

battery system An intensive egg production method that confines hens to cramped cages.

biomedical Using scientific knowledge to find ways to improve human health.

broiler chickens Hens raised for meat rather than egg laying.

bushmeat Meat of wild animals from African forests.

captive-breeding programs Human-controlled breeding programs.

companion animals Domestic or tamed animals kept for pleasure (also known as pets).

cosmetics testing Safety testing on products such as makeup, soap, tanning lotions, creams, deodorants, and shampoo.

cull To select particular animals to kill.

European Union (EU) A political, social, and economic union of 27 countries in Europe.

euthanasia Humane or painless death.

factory farming An alternative term for intensive farming.

feral A domesticated animal turned wild.

free range A non-intensive farming system that gives animals freedom of movement, outdoor access, and the opportunity to graze or forage for food.

gestation The carrying of embryos or a fetus in the womb.

indigenous Ethnic groups who have a long-standing historical connection to a particular geographical area, e.g., Aboriginals in Australia.

intensive livestock farming A highly mechanized system of farming that relies on high stocking densities, the confinement of animals, and the use of drugs and enhanced feed to produce higher yields at less cost.

invertebrates Animals without a backbone.

mastitis Serious infection causing pain and swelling in the udder of dairy cows.

osteoporosis A brittle bone disease that increases the risk of broken bones.

speciesism Prejudice by humans who assume that non-human animals are inferior species.

stock footage Images that already exist on film or video.

toxicology tests The safety testing of individual ingredients or finished products for poisons.

transgenic An animal that carries a gene or genes from another animal.

United Nations (UN) An international organization with 192 member countries that work to support issues including international law and security, economic development, health, and human rights.

vegan A person who does not eat meat or any other animal-derived foods and who also avoids the use of non-dietary animal by-products.

vegetarian A person who does not eat meat or other slaughter by-products but eats eggs, dairy, and other non-lethal animal produce.

vivisection The dissection of living animals. The term is used by the animal rights movement to refer to scientific research and safety testing on animals.

Further information

Books

Cavalieri, Paola and Peter Singer, eds. *The Great Ape Project: Equality Beyond Humanity*. St. Martin's, 1995.

Grant, Catharine. *The No-Nonsense Guide to Animal Rights*. New Internationalist, 2006.

Regan, Tom. *The Case for Animal Rights*. University of California Press, 1988, rev. ed. 2004.

Singer, Peter. *Animal Liberation*. Harper Perennial, 2001.

Stallwood, Kim, ed. *A Primer on Animal Rights: Leading Experts Write About Animal Cruelty and Exploitation*. Lantern Books, 2002.

Websites

Animal welfare websites sometimes include images of animal suffering.

www.peta.org/
   People for the Ethical Treatment of Animals website, with information, competitions, games, and celebrity news.

www.ifaw.org/ifaw/
   The International Fund for Animal Welfare website, featuring news and campaign information on animal welfare and environmental protection issues.

www.hsus.org/pets/
   The Humane Society of the United States website's pet page, with information about pet care, animal shelters, adoption and news and issues affecting pets.

www.wspc-international.org/
   The World Society for the Protection of Animals website, with news and campaign information about issues such as bullfighting and bear baiting.

www.rootsandshoots.org/
   A youth-driven network promoting positive change for animals and the environment.

Index

Entries in **bold** are for pictures.